# HENRY AND RAMONA

### From the books by
### BEVERLY CLEARY

### Adapted for the Stage

### CYNTH

**Dramatic Publishing**
Woodstock, Illinois • London, England • Melbourne, Australia

For Thomas and Doris McGean, Sam and Atticus Mowry

C.M.

*HENRY AND RAMONA* was commissioned and first produced by The Northwest Childrens Theater and School; Artistic Director, John Monteverde. It premiered May 6, 1994, at the Northwest Service Center in Portland, Oregon, under the title *HENRY HUGGINS*, with the following cast:

| | |
|---|---|
| HENRY HUGGINS | Ryan Gaughan |
| BEEZUS QUIMBY | Madeline ffitch* |
| RAMONA QUIMBY | Jane Tucker |
| MR. HUGGINS | J. Dennis Sullivan |
| MRS. HUGGINS | Lani Miller |
| SCOOTER McCARTHY | Andrew Kafoury |
| BYRON "MURPH" MURPHY | Tim Placencia |
| ROBERT KELLY | Steven Jones |
| MRS. PEABODY | Vicki Ragland-Johnson |
| MR. CAPPER | Phillip A. Rudolph |
| JUDY CAPPER | Kate Pruitt |
| ROGER | Colin Hulbert |
| MARY JANE | Katie Wilson |
| LISA | Julia Perretta |
| PAPERBOYS | Joe Kent, Sean Miller, Max Moss |
| RIBSY | Risa Davis |

| | |
|---|---|
| Director | John Monteverde |
| Stage Manager | Alison Stebbins |
| Technical Director | Charles Tyndall |
| Lighting Designer | Jeff Forbes |
| Costume Designer | Wanda Walden |
| Sound Designer | Allen Miller |
| Prop Master | Alan Ryman |
| Special "Ribsy" costume | Barbara Embree |

*Ms. ffitch spells her name with two lowercase "f"s.

# HENRY AND RAMONA

A Play in Two Acts
For 2 men, 2 women, 7-8 boys, 3-5 girls,
1 "dog" played by a child or small adult*

## CHARACTERS

HENRY HUGGINS  . . . . . . .earnest boy, almost 11 years old
SCOOTER McCARTHY  . . .boy about 13, very full of himself
ROBERT KELLY  . .enthusiastic, slightly younger than Henry
BEEZUS QUIMBY . . . . . . . . . . . . . . girl about Henry's age,
Henry's best friend, very practical
RAMONA QUIMBY  . .Beezus' younger sister, about 5 years
old, imaginative and under foot
BYRON MURPHY . . . . . . . . . . a "boy genius," Henry's age
JUDY CAPPER . . . . . . . . . . . . . . . . . . . . .a typical teenager
MAX, SEAN & JOE . . . . . . . . . paperboys, older than Henry
MARY JANE  . . . . . . . . .same age as Beezus; Beezus' friend
LISA KELLY  . . . . . . same age as Ramona; Ramona's friend
ROGER . . . . . . . . . . . . . . . . . . . . . . . boy about Henry's age
RIBSY . . . . . . . . . . . . . . . . . . . . . . . . Henry's dog, scruffy
MR. HUGGINS . . . . . . . . . . . . . . . . . . . . . . . Henry's father
MRS. HUGGINS . . . . . . . . . . . . . . . . . . . . . Henry's mother
BESSIE PEABODY . . . . . . . . . . . . . . . . . .Henry's neighbor
MR. CAPPER  . . District Manager of the *Journal* newspaper;
Judy's father

*See Production Notes.

PLACE: Klickitat Street.
TIME: The 1950s or almost any era.

# ACT ONE

## SCENE ONE

*(Springtime on Klickitat Street. Music in as SCOOTER rides onstage. Other PAPERBOYS arrive at Mr. Capper's, where a stack of papers awaits them. MARY JANE and LISA enter, sit C, and play pattycake. MR. & MRS. HUGGINS enter R, returning from a picnic. MRS. PEABODY enters, watering her flowers. ROGER and ROBERT enter, roughhousing. MRS. PEABODY douses them with the watering can. They exit. MRS. PEABODY and MR. & MRS. HUGGINS go into their houses. The PAPERBOYS exit. SCOOTER throws a paper on the Huggins' porch as he exits. Music out, lights change and HENRY enters, trying to teach RIBSY to fetch.)*

HENRY. Here, Ribsy! Ribsy!

*(RIBSY enters from doghouse.)*

HENRY. Go fetch! *(RIBSY fetches the stick and brings it into his doghouse instead of returning it to HENRY.)* You ol' dog!

*(BEEZUS enters. RAMONA trails after her, walking in a mechanical manner. She stops part-way across stage and "winds down." BEEZUS realizes RAMONA has stopped, turns, crosses to her and "winds her up.")*

7

HENRY *(watching RAMONA and BEEZUS)*. Sometimes it seems like everybody on Klickitat Street is doing stuff that doesn't make any sense. *(To BEEZUS.)* Hi, Beezus! *(BEEZUS turns, waves, and "winds-up" RAMONA again. RAMONA starts walking. HENRY turns to the audience.)* Even Beezus—and she's usually pretty sensible—for a *girl*. She's the kinda person who doesn't mind getting dirty—or digging up fishing worms. *(Looking again at the girls.)* Of course, Ramona's the worst pest on Klickitat Street. *(RAMONA salutes him. HENRY to BEEZUS again.)* What are you doing?

BEEZUS. Winding up Ramona. She's pretending to be a mechanical toy.

HENRY. Oh, brother. Don't you get tired of all that pretending?

BEEZUS. I guess. *(She has finished "winding" Ramona, who begins marching offstage while BEEZUS and HENRY talk.)*

HENRY. I'd pretend to be something important—or exciting.

BEEZUS. Like a spy? *(She strikes a spy pose.)*

HENRY. Yeah! Or a frontier scout! *(He strikes a lookout pose; then, with a look to RAMONA.)* Not some ol' wind-up doll.

RAMONA *(stopping just before exiting)*. I'm not a doll. I'm a toy soldier. *(She turns and exits, marching.)*

BEEZUS. Ramona, come back here! *(BEEZUS exits, racing to catch up with RAMONA.)*

HENRY *(getting serious again)*. I don't want to just pretend. I want to *do* something. Something important. I don't know what, but something.

*(SCOOTER has begun his paper route from the back of the theater.)*

SCOOTER. Here's your paper, Mr. Grumbie! No, sir, I didn't step in the flower beds. Yes, sir, they sure are looking fine.

HENRY. A paper route! That's it! *(He rises, demonstrating the grandeur and importance of delivering papers.)* Riding down the street on my bike tossing papers—and getting paid for it! Helping people find out what's happening every day. Now *that* makes sense! *That's* important! I could handle a paper route—easy! I'd always deliver it on time. And nobody would *ever* have to hunt around in the bushes for the paper when *I* deliver it. Nope. Perfect aim—that's me! *(He picks up the paper from the front porch and throws it. RIBSY takes it into the doghouse.)* Ribsy! And just think of all the stuff I would get with the extra money! Stamps, a flashlight—TWO flashlights! Maybe even a sleeping bag, or a new coonskin cap.

SCOOTER. Say, Huggins, I'm going to Scout Camp during spring vacation next week. Know anybody who could take my paper route while I'm gone?

HENRY. I'll take it!

SCOOTER. You're not old enough.

HENRY *(in frustration)*. I AM TOO!

SCOOTER. Mr. Capper says you've gotta be eleven years old to have a paper route.

HENRY. I feel eleven.

SCOOTER. Yes, but you *aren't* eleven.

HENRY. Come on, Scoot. I'd just be a substitute.

SCOOTER. Forget it. I can't trust some ol' fifth-grader with my route. I've got some pretty cross customers. *(Pointing to audience members.)* That old Mrs. Jones complains if just one teeny corner of her paper gets in the mud, and Mr. Grumbie gets steamed if the paper lands in his flower beds. You've gotta be careful when you deliver papers.

HENRY. Tell you what—let me take the route for one day. If I get it right without any mistakes, then I get to sub for you. Deal?

SCOOTER. I'll think about it. *(RIBSY growls.)* Mutt! *(SCOOTER exits.)*

HENRY. I *know* I can handle a paper route. I'm old enough for something important. Come on, Ribs! *(They exit.)*


## SCENE TWO

*(The next afternoon. Music up. Neighborhood activity— BEEZUS and MARY JANE enter, begin jumping rope. LISA joins them. JUDY enters, does the hula hoop. ROGER and ROBERT enter, having a squirt gun fight. SCOOTER enters and delivers papers to the Huggins' and Capper's. All exit. Music out as RIBSY enters, drops a newspaper in his doghouse, crosses to Mr. Capper's and steals another paper. HENRY enters as lights change.)*

HENRY. Here, Ribsy! *(RIBSY bounds away from the dog-house and a pile of newspapers spill out of the doghouse.)* What are all these papers doing here? *(Seeing RIBSY.)* Ribsy! *(Pause.)* Did you fetch all these papers and bring them here? You old dog. What am I gonna tell Scooter? *(He thinks for a minute, then grabs all the papers.)* Stay here, Ribsy. I've got to get these papers delivered before Scooter finds out. I bet I know the route—I've watched Scooter do it. It's not that hard. *(He begins to deliver the papers.)* Let's see—Mr. Capper gets one—I know that. And Scooter said Mrs. Jones likes hers on the front step— or was that Mr. Grumbie?

*(BEEZUS and RAMONA enter, RAMONA carrying a squirt gun. As HENRY and BEEZUS talk, RIBSY steals the papers HENRY has already re-delivered and takes them to the doghouse.)*

BEEZUS. Hi, Henry. What are you doing?

HENRY. Ribsy stole all the papers, Beezus, and I've got to deliver them again or Scooter will *never* let me take his route.

BEEZUS. I could help.

HENRY. Thanks, Beezus.

RAMONA *(squirts BEEZUS)*. You're dead.

BEEZUS. Ramona! I'm trying to help Henry. *(She grabs some papers; to HENRY.)* Where do these go?

HENRY. Well, that one can go to Mrs. Peabody. I'm sure she gets a paper. At least, I *think* she does.

*(SCOOTER rides up on his bike).*

SCOOTER. Hey! What do you think you're doing? Those are MY papers!

HENRY *(simultaneously with BEEZUS)*. Well—I—

BEEZUS. Henry was just—

SCOOTER. I knew you'd mess something up! I didn't say you could have my route yet, did I?

HENRY. I wasn't trying to take your route. It's just that Ribsy—um, I mean—

SCOOTER. Ribsy, huh? What'd you do—train that ol' mutt of yours to steal papers?

HENRY. No! I—he was just trying to help, and then I figured I knew your route and so I—

SCOOTER. Well, you didn't know my route! Mrs. Peabody doesn't get a paper—and you were gonna give her one. Somebody else's paper would've been missing.

RAMONA *(squirting SCOOTER)*. You're dead.

SCOOTER. I am not!

BEEZUS. Ramona! *(BEEZUS drops papers while trying to get RAMONA out of the way.)*

SCOOTER *(turning to HENRY)*. I suppose you're going to let Ribsy steal my papers all the time and make me lose my route.

HENRY. No. I'll untrain him.

RAMONA *(squirts HENRY with the squirt gun)*. You're dead.

HENRY. Aw, cut it out!

BEEZUS. Ramona!

SCOOTER. You better untrain him. And I'm going to find somebody else to take my route while I'm gone, too.

BEEZUS. Henry can handle your route.

SCOOTER. I have enough trouble with papers getting in the mud and stuff without having some old mutt going around stealing them.

HENRY. I could've delivered them again before anybody complained.

SCOOTER. Sure—to all the wrong people. And you had to get a *girl* to help you.

BEEZUS. So?

HENRY. Beezus isn't a girl—she's my friend.

SCOOTER. It doesn't matter. You can't fill in when I'm gone.

HENRY. Come on, Scoot. Give me a chance. You give me your route book and let me deliver your papers tomorrow. If I do it right and Ribsy doesn't take any, I get the route while you're gone. How about it?

BEEZUS. It seems fair to me.

SCOOTER *(glaring at her)*. OK. I s'pose that'll make you untrain him all right. But you just remember, if you make me lose my route, I'll, I'll...Well, I'll do something. *(He exits with his papers. BEEZUS drags RAMONA out, HENRY drags RIBSY out. Both are being scolded.)*

HENRY. Come on, Ribsy! Inside—NOW! Bad dog!


## SCENE THREE

*(The following day. Music up. The PAPERBOYS arrive. MRS. PEABODY enters from audience, handing out flyers advertising a rummage sale.)*

MRS. PEABODY *(ad libs as she's handing out flyers)*. Spring cleaning! Time for a rummage sale! Have a flyer! Bring over your old knickknacks to sell. The more the merrier! Be sure to stop by and browse. Who knows what treasures you'll find! *(Etc. She reaches the stage, gives flyers to the PAPERBOYS, stops to chat with MRS. HUGGINS, and MR. HUGGINS as he returns from work. JUDY enters, drawing all the attention. She hands a large stack of newspapers to the PAPERBOYS, whispers to one of them, exits. PAPERBOYS react. All PAPERBOYS except SCOOTER finish counting papers and exit. Music out. HENRY enters with a newspaper, chased by RIBSY. They engage in a tug of war over the newspaper. RAMONA and BEEZUS enter, RAMONA still carrying her squirt gun.)*

BEEZUS. Thought of a way to get Ribsy untrained yet?

HENRY. No. I've tried everything.

RAMONA *(squirting HENRY)*. You're dead!

HENRY. I am not dead. I can't be dead if I'm not playing, can I?

SCOOTER *(crosses to them with his bag of newspapers and gives them to HENRY)*. I better not get any complaints about missing papers today or *any other day.*

HENRY *(half-heartedly)*. You won't.

SCOOTER. I better not!

RAMONA *(squirts him)*. You're dead.

SCOOTER. Pest! *(SCOOTER exits.)*

BEEZUS *(addressing HENRY)*. I don't care what Scooter says about girls. I'm helping you. *(HENRY and BEEZUS begin counting newspapers. RIBSY snatches one up in his mouth.)*

HENRY. Ribsy! Drop that! *(He grabs the paper and they begin their tug of war. RAMONA squirts RIBSY.)*

RAMONA. You're dead! *(RIBSY drops the paper and whimpers.)*

HENRY. Hey! Did you see that? Ramona made him drop the paper! Do it again, Ramona.

RAMONA. No.

HENRY. Aw, come on, Ramona, squirt Ribsy again. This has just got to work.

RAMONA. No.

BEEZUS *(coaxing)*. Ramona, can I have the squirt gun?

RAMONA. It's MINE!

SCOOTER *(from offstage)*. Huggins! You better get going delivering those papers!

*(HENRY runs inside. BEEZUS chases RAMONA. JUDY enters, settles down to read and watch the goings on.)*

RAMONA. MINE! Mine-mine-mine-mine-mine-mine-mine-mine!

*(HENRY returns with a squirt gun of his own just as BEEZUS wrestles the other squirt gun away from RA-MONA. HENRY throws a paper to RIBSY.)*

HENRY. Fetch, Ribsy! *(As RIBSY goes to pick up the paper, HENRY squirts him. RIBSY drops the paper.)*

RAMONA. You're dead! *(She claps her hands.)*

HENRY. It works! I'm going to get Ribsy untrained after all! Come on. Let's go.

BEEZUS *(waving the squirt gun and facing off with RIBSY).* I'll keep you covered! *(They exit, RAMONA last, skipping and clapping. Lights change.)*

## SCENE FOUR

*(Later the same evening. Music up. MR. CAPPER enters and hands JUDY a pail and sponge to wash the windows. SCOOTER enters, shows off on his bike for JUDY, gets off to talk with her. JUDY hands the sponge over to him and he takes over washing the windows. MARY JANE enters, talks to JUDY. They exit. ROGER and ROBERT enter, play with Scooter's bike. SCOOTER realizes JUDY is gone, chases ROGER and ROBERT away and plants himself on the Huggins' porch in dismay. Music out. BEEZUS, HENRY, RAMONA and RIBSY re-enter. HENRY carries the empty newspaper bag. SCOOTER immediately assumes his "superior seventh-grader" attitude.)*

SCOOTER. How many did your mutt run off with?

HENRY. He isn't a mutt and he didn't run off with any. He wouldn't touch a paper, see? *(He throws a paper. RIBSY ignores it.)* I guess I did a pretty good job of delivering papers. You won't get any complaints tonight.

BEEZUS. We double-checked every address on the list.

HENRY. And now I get to deliver papers while you're away, right?

SCOOTER. Sure, if you don't think it's too much hard work for a fifth-grader.

HENRY. You just wait. I'm practically eleven already.

SCOOTER. Ha! *(He gets on his bike and begins to leave.)*

RAMONA *(squirting him and chasing offstage after him).* You're dead!

SCOOTER. Buzz off!

BEEZUS. Ramona! *(She runs offstage after RAMONA. HENRY picks up the newspaper from his front porch, tosses it with a satisfied air and exits.)*


SCENE FIVE


*(Mrs. Peabody's rummage sale! Music up. MRS. PEA-BODY enters and puts up a "Rummage Sale" sign in front of her house. PAPERBOYS enter, helping MRS. PEABODY carry on several large boxes, one containing an electric fan. MR. CAPPER enters, crosses to Mrs. Peabody's. ROGER, MARY JANE and LISA enter, playing tag and descending on MR. CAPPER. MR. CAPPER makes a purchase, departs, again with the tag-players swarming around him. SCOOTER and HENRY enter, arguing. HENRY wears a jacket. As the crowd leaves and music goes out, SCOOTER fires his parting shot to HENRY.)*

SCOOTER. I told you, Huggins. You're not old enough!
    *(HENRY sits on the porch with RIBSY, disappointed.)*
JUDY. Old enough for what?
SCOOTER. Huh? *(Turns and sees JUDY).* Oh, ah—um...
    newspapers! Hi, Judy.
JUDY. Hi, Scooter.
SCOOTER. Yeah. Ol' Henry thinks he can handle the new
    paper route. But you gotta be pret-ty responsible to have a
    paper route.
JUDY. Uh-huh.
SCOOTER. I've got a paper route, you know.
JUDY. Yes, I know.
SCOOTER. Yup. It's hard work, delivering papers.
JUDY. Guess so.
SCOOTER. Yeah, well. Guess I better get going. Delivering
    those papers. Hard work. Um... see ya, Judy.
JUDY. Bye. *(She waves. SCOOTER exits. JUDY and MRS.
    PEABODY exit.)*
HENRY *(to RIBSY).* Scooter's such a big show-off. Just
    'cause he's in the seventh grade. I'm plenty old enough for
    my own paper route. I delivered his papers, didn't I? I'll
    show him. I'll march right up to Mr. Capper's house—I'll
    just march right up—and—and I'll ask him for a paper
    route, that's what I'll do. I'll be so businesslike he won't
    even *ask* my age. And anyway, I'm *practically* eleven. *(He
    turns to RIBSY.)* How do you do? I'm Henry Huggins. I
    heard you were looking for a paper boy. *(He shakes his
    head, tries again.)* Good afternoon. My name is Henry
    Huggins. I understand you are looking for a boy to *deliver
    papers. (He smooths his hair down, straightens his shirt,
    etc.)* Y'know, Ribs, I'll bet Mr. Capper won't even have to
    ask what I want. One look at me and he'll *know* I mean
    business. *(Now becoming MR. CAPPER.)* Young man, do

you want a job? *(Now HENRY again.)* Yes, sir. No need to convince me, sir. I'll be glad to take the job, sir. *(He smiles, pleased with himself. Then addresses the bushes with an air of importance.)* Sorry, guys. Can't play ball with you now. I have to start my paper route. *(He breathes a contented sigh.)* MY PAPER ROUTE. *(Turning to RIBSY.)* Now, Ribsy, you stay here. I can't have some ol' dog following me when I go to see Mr. Capper. It isn't very businesslike. Go on. Go home! *(RIBSY exits.)*

*(MRS. PEABODY enters from the back gate carrying box of "kittens.")*

MRS. PEABODY. Well, well—Harry Higgins! How are you today?

HENRY. I'm all right, Mrs. Peabody. *(Crosses to her, reading the sign.)* A rummage sale? You mean you want to get rid of all this great stuff?

MRS. PEABODY. Well, it's time for some new "stuff."

HENRY *(poking around in the various boxes)*. How much for the electric fan?

MRS. PEABODY. Twenty-five cents.

HENRY *(looking the fan over carefully)*. Could you hold it for me for about half an hour?

MRS. PEABODY. I'm sorry, Harry, but if someone else wants it while you're gone, I'll have to sell it.

HENRY. Oh. *(Pause; to audience.)* I better not buy it—I wouldn't look very businesslike carrying an electric fan. *(To MRS. PEABODY.)* What do you do with the stuff no one wants?

MRS. PEABODY *(with relish)*. Take it TO THE DUMP! *(Poking around, HENRY spots the "kittens" box.)*

HENRY. Kittens! *(From here on, "meows" are intermittently heard.)* But kittens aren't junk! They're not for sale, are they?

MRS. PEABODY. I'm afraid so. Fifteen cents apiece.

HENRY. If nobody buys them, will they go to the dump, too?

MRS. PEABODY *(chuckles)*. No. I suppose they'll go to the pound.

HENRY. I don't think you should let them go to the pound.

MRS. PEABODY. Well, I certainly can't keep them. I'm getting a new dog, you know.

HENRY. Really?

MRS. PEABODY. Yes. His name's Ranger. Now, you know four kittens and a brand new dog just wouldn't get along.

HENRY. I guess not.

MRS. PEABODY. I'll tell you what. I can let you have them for five cents apiece.

HENRY. A nickel a kitten! That's a bargain! But carrying a box of kittens wouldn't be very businesslike. *(A "meow" is heard.)* They *are* awfully nice. *(He fingers the zipper on his jacket, thinks for a minute.)* I'll take all four. *(He pays MRS. PEABODY and gently places the four "kittens" inside his jacket.)*

MRS. PEABODY. Are you sure you don't want to carry them in the box? Four kittens is a lot to carry in your jacket.

HENRY. If I'm going to ask Mr. Capper for a paper route, I've got to look businesslike. Thanks anyway, Mrs. Peabody. *(He squirms, wriggles, pats his middle and heads to Mr. Capper's house, straightening his hair and pushing the "kittens" back down and out of sight. Nervously practicing.)* Good afternoon, Mr. Cooper—ah, Capper. Good afternoon, Mr. Capper. My name is Harry Higgins—uh, Henry Hoogins. Henry Huggins. My name is Henry Huggins.

*(HENRY walks over to the Capper's, rehearsing his speech to himself. He knocks on the door. JUDY answers.)*

JUDY. Yeah?

HENRY *(turning to JUDY)*. Good afternoon, Mr.—Uh...uh, is Mr. Capper home?

JUDY. Hang on. *(Yelling inside.)* DA-A-A-A-AD!! SOME BOY WANTS TO SEE YOU!

*(MR. CAPPER appears in the doorway.)*

MR. CAPPER. Hello there. What can I do for you?

HENRY. Good afternoon. My name...*(He twitches, looks down at his jacket.)* My name...*(A "meow" is heard. HENRY fidgets to keep the "kittens" from escaping; then, quickly.)* MynameisHenryHuggins!

MR. CAPPER *(amused)*. How do you do? *(He moves to shake hands. Both HENRY's hands are occupied with holding his jacket closed.)*

HENRY *(still holding onto his jacket)*. How do you do? No! I mean OW! *(Another "meow." HENRY looks down at the "kittens.")*

MR. CAPPER. What have you got in your jacket, son?

HENRY. Uh...um...*(Struggling with his jacket.)* Nothing. *(A "meow.")* Um, that is—*(He tries to sound nonchalant.)* Just some kittens. *(JUDY giggles. HENRY looks desperate, finally blurts out.)* Mr. Capper, could I have a paper route?

MR. CAPPER. You're a little young for a paper route, sonny.

HENRY. I'm real responsible...I can ride a bike and throw straight and...things.

MR. CAPPER. There's more to a paper route than riding a bike and throwing papers. You have to be able to handle money and deliver the papers on time in every kind of weather.

HENRY (*a meow*). OUCH!! (*To MR. CAPPER.*) Um, I mean, I'm sure I can do all that.

MR. CAPPER. It takes a special kind of person to deliver the news, you know. Where would this country be today without the Pony Express? No, my boy, not everyone can deliver the newspaper. Come back in a few years.

HENRY (*disappointed*). Well...thanks just the same. (*He turns to leave. A meow.*)

JUDY (*as MR. CAPPER closes the door*). Carrying kittens around in a jacket! I could just die!

(*MR. and MRS. HUGGINS enter and sit on the porch.*)

HENRY (*to the audience*). Well, at least I've still got the kittens. You've gotta admit they're pretty neat. (*A meow.*) OW! Mom! Dad! Guess what I've got?! (*MR. and MRS. HUGGINS exchange glances.*)

MRS. HUGGINS. I can't imagine.

HENRY (*beaming*). Kittens! (*He begins taking them out of the jacket and handing them to MRS. HUGGINS, who, in turn, hands them to MR. HUGGINS.*)

MRS. HUGGINS. Oh, Henry!

HENRY. Four of them! They're really nice!

MRS. HUGGINS. Henry, I don't know how you come up with these ideas. (*With a look to MR. HUGGINS.*) It-must be something you inherit from your father. (*She exits into the house.*)

MR. HUGGINS (*calling inside after her*). He certainly didn't get it from *me*. Nobody in *my* family ever brought kittens home in their jacket.

HENRY. I bought them at Mrs. Peabody's rummage sale. She was selling them with all the other junk. Only a nickel apiece! They were going to go to the pound.

MR. HUGGINS. So you rescued them, eh?

HENRY. Uh-huh.

*(MRS. HUGGINS has returned with the picnic basket. She places the kittens inside.)*

MRS. HUGGINS. That was very... noble of you, Henry.

MR. HUGGINS. Well, you can't keep all *four* of them...

MRS. HUGGINS *(with a look to her husband)*. You can't keep any of them.

HENRY. But—

MR. HUGGINS. Pets are a big responsibility, Henry.

HENRY. Aw, Dad—I could handle it.

MR. HUGGINS. Maybe when you're older we could talk about another pet. But I'd say Ribsy is plenty for now—too much sometimes. Tomorrow morning, take the kittens down to the pet shop and give them to Mr. Pennycuff.

HENRY. But, I don't want them sold to strangers. I want them to have good homes. *(After a moment.)* Can't I sell them around the neighborhood myself? *(Showing off his sales technique.)* Special offer! Today only! Free kittens with every newspaper subscription! Without cost or obligation! While supplies last!

MR. HUGGINS. You have the makings of a fine salesman, Henry. But for now, I think we'll leave the selling to Mr. Pennycuff.

HENRY. Aw, shucks!

MRS. HUGGINS. Henry!

MR. HUGGINS. Young man!

## SCENE SIX

*(Late summer. Music up. MRS. PEABODY enters, beckons MR. HUGGINS to help her move the rummage sale boxes offstage. MRS. HUGGINS decorates the house for HENRY's birthday. Kids arrive, bringing presents. MR. HUGGINS wheels a bike with a big bow into the front yard. He exits with MRS. HUGGINS and RIBSY. Music out. We hear kids singing to HENRY: "Happy birthday, dear Henry. Happy birthday to you!!" They cheer. HENRY and ROBERT enter.)*

ROBERT. So, what did you get for your birthday, Henry?

HENRY. Three flashlights, two packs of stamps, a model airplane and two puzzles—AND Dad helped me pay for this keen new bike! But the best part is I'm old enough for a paper route—if I can get one.

ROBERT. Well, you did a good job when you took over for Scooter.

HENRY. Don't tell anybody, but I heard Chuck's quitting. Maybe I'll get his route, if nobody else gets it first. *(HENRY wheels his bike to the side of the house.)*

ROBERT. Keen! I won't tell anybody—promise!

*(MURPH enters and begins working on Thorvo, the robot.)*

ROBERT. Hey—look! It's the new kid. What d'you s'pose he's doing?

HENRY. Look at all those wires! You could make your own phone system with all that stuff.

ROBERT. Like a private line!

HENRY *(going up to MURPH)*. Hi! Are you the new boy?

MURPH. Yup.

HENRY. My name's Henry. (*A pause. No answer from MURPH, who is deep into his work.*) This is Robert. (*Another pause.*) What's your name?

MURPH. Byron Murphy.

ROBERT (*smothering a giggle*). Byron?!

MURPH (*giving ROBERT a look*). Call me Murph.

HENRY. Okay, Murph. You sure have a lot of wires and stuff. Want to rig up a phone line between our houses?

ROBERT (*rapidly, excitedly*). We could string it over the fences and through the trees and hook up your house and Henry's house and my house!

MURPH. Why couldn't we just call each other?

ROBERT. You mean—on the regular phone? The one that belongs to the phone company?

MURPH. Sure. (*HENRY and ROBERT exchange glances.*)

HENRY (*disappointed*). Well, I guess we could. We just thought it would be fun. (*MURPH exits, returns with the rest of Thorvo, the robot.*) I live right next door. You could come over and play checkers if you want.

MURPH (*with a withering look*). I play chess.

HENRY. Oh...well, I'll be too busy to play games pretty soon, anyway, with my paper route and all.

MURPH. A paper route keeps you busy all right. I've got one in my old neighborhood.

HENRY. You do?

ROBERT. Henry's gonna have his own route, too, pretty soon. See, Chuck's quitting and then Henry's gonna get his route. (*HENRY pokes ROBERT for spilling the beans.*)

MURPH (*interested*). Really?

HENRY. *Maybe.* (*Quickly changing the subject.*) So, what're you building?

MURPH. A robot.

ROBERT. A robot?

MURPH. Sure. See? *(He shows them the robot so far.)*

HENRY. If you put a funnel upside down on his head, he'd look like the Tin Man from the *Wizard of* Oz.

MURPH. This isn't any Tin Man.

ROBERT. Do you really expect it to work?

MURPH. Sure. I've got it all figured out, with batteries and magnets and stuff. Maybe even a record player inside so he can talk.

ROBERT. Wow! A robot that can talk! You must be some kind of genius!

*(BEEZUS and RAMONA enter from HENRY's house, having just been at the birthday party. RAMONA is playing dress-up and clonking around in a pair of women's red high-heels.)*

BEEZUS. Happy birthday, Henry!

HENRY. Thanks, Beezus.

RAMONA *(singing)*. Happy birthday to you! You live in a zoo! You look like a monkey, and you smell like one, too!

BEEZUS. Ramona!

HENRY. Beezus, this is Murph.

MURPH *(looking up for a moment and grunting)*. Hi. *(MURPH goes back to work, not waiting for a reply. RAMONA follows Murph around, gets into his wires, etc.)*

ROBERT. He's building a talking robot!

BEEZUS. No kidding! *(After a moment.)* If you put a funnel on him for a hat, he'd look like the Tin—

ROBERT *(cutting off BEEZUS)*. Shhh!

BEEZUS. Does he have a name?

MURPH *(rolling his eyes)*. Thorvo.

HENRY *(attempting to include BEEZUS and soften MURPH's contempt)*. Good name.

ROBERT. What are you going to use for his legs?

MURPH. Pipes, if I can find some.

HENRY. There's a plumber over by the supermarket. I bet he'd give you some pipes.

BEEZUS. Are his eyes going to light up?

MURPH. Of course.

BEEZUS. If you put in blue bulbs, he could have blue eyes!

MURPH (*with contempt*). Thorvo's eyes are red and they're staying that way.

RAMONA. I think red eyes are pretty!

BEEZUS. Shh!

RAMONA (*stands next to MURPH, watching him work, begins singing to herself, getting louder as she goes*). A, B, C, D, E, F, G! H, I, J, K, LMNOP! Q, R, S—!

BEEZUS. Ramona, don't be such a nuisance!

RAMONA (*lunging toward MURPH, trying to grab his glasses*). I want glasses like he has.

BEEZUS (*restraining her*). You don't need glasses.

RAMONA. But I want them!

MURPH. How am I supposed to get anything done with all these girls around? (*He starts to pack up Thorvo.*)

HENRY (*pleading*). Aw, come on, Murph. Beezus is all right.

MURPH. She's a girl. (*He stalks off, carrying Thorvo.*)

BEEZUS (*to RAMONA*). Now see what you did?

RAMONA. I did NOT!

BEEZUS. Wait 'til Mother hears what a pest you are!

RAMONA. I am NOT a pest!

BEEZUS. You are too! You're the biggest pest on Klickitat Street! (*They exit, arguing.*)

HENRY (*calling after them*). Sorry, Beezus.

ROBERT (*looking back towards MURPH's exit with awe*). A real live genius, right here on Klickitat Street! Wow! (*ROBERT and HENRY exit*).

## SCENE SEVEN

*(Fourth of July. Music up. MR. HUGGINS is mowing the lawn. MR. CAPPER enters, puts up a small American flag. The PAPERBOYS arrive. MAX and SEAN talk, exit through Mrs. Peabody's back gate. MRS. HUGGINS enters, puts up a small American flag, gives MR. HUGGINS a glass of lemonade. MR. HUGGINS takes a break from lawn mowing. RAMONA enters, waving an American flag and shouting "God Bless America!" BEEZUS chases after her, takes the flag, starts talking with SCOOTER and JOE. RAMONA steals the flag from the Huggins' porch and races off, followed by BEEZUS. Sounds of fire crackers. MAX and SEAN race on from Mrs. Peabody's yard, laughing. MRS. PEABODY chases them off with her broom. JUDY enters, hands the newspapers to the PAPERBOYS. They wave. MR. CAPPER enters and sends JUDY back inside. THE PAPERBOYS get back to business. Music out. HENRY enters.)*

HENRY. Say, Mr. Capper.

MR. CAPPER. Yes, Henry?

HENRY. Did you know my birthday was last week?

MR. CAPPER. Was it? Well, happy birthday, Henry!

HENRY. Thanks. I was just wondering—I heard Chuck was quitting and, um, now that I'm eleven and all I thought maybe I could have his route. *(The other boys are listening expectantly.)*

MR. CAPPER. I'm afraid not, Henry.

HENRY. I-I can't?

MR. CAPPER. Sorry, son.

HENRY. But I thought you needed someone to take over for Chuck.

MR. CAPPER. I did. But one of the district managers phoned me about a real whiz-kid in his district who wanted to shift to this neighborhood. Experience and brains, my boy. That's the ticket. But you keep up the good work.

HENRY. Would you mind telling me the name of the new carrier?

MR. CAPPER. Let's see...Boyd? "B" something—Byron?

HENRY. Byron Murphy?!

MR. CAPPER. That's the fella. Know him?

HENRY. Sort of.

MR. CAPPER. Don't you worry, Henry. You'll get your chance. I know you're no quitter. *(MR. CAPPER pats HENRY on the shoulder. To the rest of the PAPERBOYS.)* All right, folks! Let's get those papers delivered! The headlines can't wait, you know! *(MR. CAPPER exits. The PAPERBOYS pat HENRY on the shoulder to console him— "Tough break, Henry." PAPERBOYS exit.)*

HENRY. Ha! Some friend *Murph* turned out to be! I guess a *genius* can do anything. It's not fair! Wish he hadn't even moved into our neighborhood. I hope his old robot doesn't work at all! *(He sits dejectedly an the porch. Lights change.)*

## SCENE EIGHT

*(A barbecue at Mr. Capper's house. Music up. MR. CAPPER enters, sets up a card table in front of his house. MR. and MRS. HUGGINS enter, with food and a tablecloth. They console HENRY, cross to Mr. Capper's. MRS. PEABODY enters, crosses to Mr. Capper's, bringing food for the picnic. RIBSY enters, puts his head on HENRY's lap. Two PAPERBOYS ride by, wave to HENRY, who watches*

*sadly. Music out as RAMONA enters, wearing a pair of glasses, frames tied with a string in the back to keep them on. She skips by, her hands full of newspapers.)*

RAMONA *(handing HENRY a newspaper).* Hello.

*(HENRY watches her pass, puzzled. MURPH enters.)*

MURPH. Hey! You come back with my newspapers! *(MURPH and RAMONA engage in a chase up and down the aisles. Neighbors and kids gather to watch. General hubbub and noise. The following lines happen simultaneously.)*

HENRY. Hey, Mr. Capper! Look!

MR. CAPPER. Byron! Byron Murphy! What are you doing! Your route's not on this street!

MRS. HUGGINS. Oh my goodness! Ramona! Does your mother know where you are?

MRS. PEABODY. Young man, stop picking on that poor little girl! And watch out for Mr. Grumbie's flower beds!

MR. HUGGINS. Look out! She's right behind you!

MURPH *(catches up with RAMONA as they get back onstage. Adult hubbub stops).* Give me those papers right now!

RAMONA. No! I want to deliver them! I'm a paper boy! *(MURPH grabs the papers. He and RAMONA engage in a tug of war.)* You give me back my papers!

MURPH. They aren't your papers.

RAMONA *(begins throwing a tantrum).* Mine! Mine-mine-mine-mine-mine-mine-mine!

*(BEEZUS enters, running.)*

BEEZUS. Ramona! Get off the ground! *(RAMONA screams and kicks.)* I'm sorry, Murph. I don't know how she got away.

MURPH *(angrily)*. Yeah. Thanks a lot. *(He takes his papers and exits.)*

HENRY *(to BEEZUS, who is trying to haul RAMONA offstage)*. Need any help?

BEEZUS. I don't know what'll do any good.

RAMONA. I'm a paper boy.

HENRY *(enjoying it a little)*. She sure gave old Murph a bad time.

BEEZUS *(rolling her eyes as she and RAMONA exit)*. You know how Ramona is when she starts pretending.

HENRY. I know. Well, I guess Murph will figure out how to handle it. *(To himself.)* After all, he is a genius. *(He exits. A thunderclap ends the neighborhood barbecue. ADULTS exit into Mr. Capper's house to get dry as transition music starts.)*


SCENE NINE

*(A rainy, cloudy day in early fall. MARY JANE enters with an umbrella. LISA runs ahead of her, no umbrella, catching raindrops on her tongue. ROGER and ROBERT enter, dueling with their umbrellas. MAX and JUDY enter. He's walking her home from school. He holds the umbrella for her as she enters the house. He turns, sighs, exits. Music out as HENRY enters. MURPH enters with a Journal bag full of papers.)*


MURPH *(to HENRY)*. You can have the route.

HENRY. What?!

MURPH. I said, you can have the route.

HENRY. You mean you don't want it?

MURPH. No.

HENRY *(suspiciously)*. How come?

MURPH. Ramona.

HENRY. Ramona?! She's just a little kid!

MURPH. I know, but she can sure make a lot of trouble.

HENRY. I'm not so sure Mr. Capper wants me to have a route.

MURPH. Yes he does.

HENRY. How do you know?

MURPH. I asked him. *(Pause.)* I guess I shouldn't have taken the route when I knew you wanted it, but I just had to. My other route was too far away and I needed money to buy parts for Thorvo. Dad thinks Thorvo's a waste of time, so I have to pay for the parts myself. But Ramona's making so much trouble I prob'ly would've lost the route, anyway.

HENRY. OK, Murph, I'll take the route.

MURPH *(relieved)*. Thanks. Here's the route book and the papers. *(He hands HENRY the Journal bag.)*

HENRY. Murph...does your dad really think Thorvo's a waste of time?

MURPH. Yeah. I guess I'll have to put all that stuff away 'til I figure out how to pay for parts. *(Pause.)* If you still want to make that private phone line, I have most of the stuff. And I already know how to build one.

HENRY. You do?

MURPH. Sure.

HENRY. Okay.

MURPH. Guess I'll see ya around. Good luck with the route.

HENRY. Thanks. *(MURPH exits.)* Imagine! A genius licked by a five-year-old! She's just a kindergartner. I'm not gonna let her stand in my way! Maybe I'm no genius, but I'm still smarter than a five-year-old.

*(He goes to get his bike. RAMONA enters and sits down.)*

RAMONA. Hello.

HENRY. Hello, Ramona. *(He begins to deliver papers. RAMONA follows after him, picking up all his papers. HENRY spots her.)* Hey, cut that out! Give me those!

RAMONA. No! I'm going to deliver them!

*(She and HENRY have a tug of war. He grabs the papers, she begins a tantrum. BEEZUS enters.)*

BEEZUS. Ramona! You're supposed to be in the house!

RAMONA *(grabbing HENRY in an attempt to get the papers back)*. I'm a paperboy—like Henry and Murph!

HENRY. Get off me, will ya?

BEEZUS *(prying RAMONA free from HENRY)*. I'm sorry, Henry. *(RAMONA is wailing.)* Ramona, be *quiet!* *(To HENRY.)* Mom says she has to stay in her room 'til the papers are delivered, but she keeps getting out.

HENRY. We've got to do something or I'll lose my route.

BEEZUS. We've tried, but when we don't want her to do something, she just wants to do it even more. The only way I can ever get her to do what I want is by getting her to pretend...wait a minute—! *(BEEZUS and HENRY look at each other and get an idea. They whisper together. RAMONA is now trying to listen in, pleased to be the center of attention.)*

HENRY. I know just the thing. Hang onto Ramona, Beezus.

BEEZUS. Gotcha. *(HENRY exits behind his house.)*

RAMONA. Where's Henry going?

BEEZUS. You'll see.

RAMONA. I want to go TOO!

BEEZUS. Ramona, how do you know you want to go if you don't know where he's going?!

RAMONA. But I WANT to go!

BEEZUS. Let's pretend we're waiting for a bus. When Henry comes back, that means the bus is here. Okay?

RAMONA. Henry's not a bus, he's a paperboy.

*(HENRY returns with a big cardboard box made into a makeshift robot head.)*

HENRY. Hey, Ramona—how would you like to be a robot like Thorvo? *(RAMONA nods excitedly).* Now, remember. A robot can't move very fast and it jerks along when it walks. *(He places the cardboard box over RAMONA's head.)*

RAMONA. Clank, clank. *(She begins walking, slowly and jerkily, like a robot.)*

BEEZUS. And a robot can't bend at the waist because it doesn't have any waist!

RAMONA. Clank.

BEEZUS. Henry, you're a genius!

HENRY. You're the one who thought of pretending.

BEEZUS. That's true. Well, guess you've got some papers to deliver.

HENRY. Yup. I better get going. *(He begins to leave. RA-MONA waves at him as a robot.)*

RAMONA. Clank, clank!

HENRY. Clank, clank, Ramona! *(HENRY exits. RAMONA clanks out with BEEZUS.)*

## SCENE TEN

*(A Saturday in the late fall. JUDY enters, turns on the radio. Music up. PAPERBOYS arrive, drawn to the music, and dance the jitterbug with JUDY, one by one. SCOOTER is last and really hams it up. During the dancing, HENRY, BEEZUS and RIBSY enter from Henry's house. MR. CAPPER enters, turns off the music. Music out. JUDY turns and sees him— "Daaaad!" She exits, MR. CAPPER follows, then PAPERBOYS, in a different direction. MRS. PEABODY enters from the back gate, pushing a hand-truck/dolly with an old bathtub on it.)*

MRS. PEABODY. Whew! These old bathtubs were built like battleships! *(She heads back inside for some more junk.)*

BEEZUS. I wonder what she's doing with that.

HENRY. Maybe she doesn't want to take baths anymore. *(They giggle.)*

*(JUDY enters, settles down on Mr. Capper's porch to read. MRS. PEABODY re-enters, carrying a box of odds and ends, which she puts inside the bathtub.)*

HENRY. Say, Mrs. Peabody, what are you going to do with that tub?

MRS. PEABODY *(with an exhilarated air)*. Take it to the dump!

BEEZUS. To the dump?

MRS. PEABODY. Unless *you'd* like to have it. Spring cleaning, you know!

BEEZUS. But it's fall!

MRS. PEABODY. Better late than never. Besides, I like spring-time best. Well, one more load to go! *(She exits again.)*

BEEZUS. Too bad she's getting rid of it. That's a pretty keen bathtub.

HENRY. Sure is. Just think of all the stuff you could use it for. A bathtub in the front yard would be a lot more fun than one in the bathroom. *(As they come up with ideas, HENRY and BEEZUS begin pushing the dolly, climbing in the tub, etc. JUDY watches them, amused.)*

BEEZUS. It could be a swimming pool when it's hot out.

HENRY. We could use it to give Ribsy a bath!

BEEZUS. Yeah! Or bob for apples on Halloween!

HENRY. Or build a clubhouse around it—if we had enough lumber.

BEEZUS *(finding an old beat-up umbrella)*. Hey, Henry! I'm captain of a submarine! Up periscope! *(She opens the umbrella as HENRY pushes her, in the bathtub, across the stage.)*

HENRY. Dive! Dive! *(They reach the other end of the stage. BEEZUS climbs out of the bathtub. HENRY pulls an old straw hat with a red, white and blue band out of the bathtub.)* Look, Beezus! I'm the President! *(He climbs into the tub, waves regally.)*

BEEZUS *(pushing HENRY along)*. It's the Fourth of July parade! *(HENRY sits up straight, nods, waves, etc., acting Presidential.)* Hats off! The flag is passing by!

JUDY. Hey! Don't forget to wash your back, Mr. President! *(She laughs.)*

*(MRS. PEABODY enters with her last box of stuff.)*

MRS. PEABODY *(looking at the kids and the bathtub)*. How would you two like to ride to the dump with me?

HENRY *(exchanging looks with BEEZUS)*. Could we ride in
the bathtub?
MRS. PEABODY. Why not?
HENRY & BEEZUS. Great!
MRS. PEABODY *(pulling out the beat-up umbrella and
using it like a parade leader's staff)*. Follow me! *(All three
exit. MRS. PEABODY in the lead, holding the umbrella
aloft, HENRY in the tub, saluting, BEEZUS behind, pushing. RIBSY exits into doghouse. Blackout.)*

## END ACT ONE

# ACT TWO

## SCENE ONE

*(Later the same day. Music indicating the passage of time. MRS. HUGGINS enters, looking for HENRY, exits around side of house. The PAPERBOYS arrive, wondering where HENRY is. Judy's music plays, PAPERBOYS wait expectantly, only to be disappointed by the arrival of MR. CAPPER in place of JUDY. He hands over the papers and the BOYS begin counting them. MR. CAPPER is checking his watch, counting out papers. The PAPERBOYS leave. Music out as MRS. HUGGINS enters from back gate, with Henry's bike and* Journal *bag.)*

MRS. HUGGINS. Henry? He-e-e-n-n-r-y! Now where has he gotten to? He should have started his paper route by now.

MR. CAPPER *(walks over with papers and a route book)*. Henry hasn't picked up his papers yet.

MRS. HUGGINS. Oh, Mr. Capper. I can't imagine where he is.

MR. CAPPER. Well, the other boys can't deliver his papers along with their own. I'm afraid his customers aren't going to be very happy. The headlines can't wait, you know.

MRS. HUGGINS. I'm sure Henry will be back soon. I'll see that the papers get delivered.

MR. CAPPER. That's the spirit! Here's his papers and a copy of his route. Good luck!

MRS. HUGGINS. Thank you. *(To herself.)* Honestly, sometimes that boy—!

*(MRS. HUGGINS picks up the papers and begins the route around the theater, throwing the papers rather awkwardly. SEAN and MAX enter, watching her.)*

SEAN. Say, isn't that Henry's mom?

MAX. It sure is!

SEAN. Look at her throw! *(They mimic MRS. HUGGINS throwing. MR. CAPPER catches them at it.)*

MR. CAPPER. I trust you boys aren't mocking a fellow news carrier.

SEAN & MAX. Uh—No, sir, Mr. Capper.

MR. CAPPER. I should hope not. You've got to respect the pinch hitters, you know. Sometimes the game depends on them.

SEAN & MAX. Yes, sir.

MR. CAPPER. Now, you boys worry about your own routes. No broken windows and no muddy papers!

SEAN & MAX *(hurrying off)*. Yes, sir!

MR. CAPPER. Off you go!

*(MR. HUGGINS enters from the street, just returning from work. He stops short, peers into the distance with a puzzled look.)*

MR. HUGGINS. What in the world—?!

MR. CAPPER. Your wife is a credit to the news profession, my friend. A credit to the profession!

MR. HUGGINS *(still puzzled)*. I'm sure she'll be pleased to hear that.

MR. CAPPER *(as he and MR. HUGGINS cross to his porch)*. No finer calling in the world!

MRS. HUGGINS *(from the theater)*. Oh, dear—I'm terribly sorry, Mr. Grumbie! No, I don't make it a habit of murder-

ing innocent flowers, Mr. Grumbie. Yes, I know they make
the world a more beautiful place.

*(HENRY and BEEZUS come running onstage, out of
breath.)*

BEEZUS. Henry, is that your mother over there?
HENRY. Oh no! *(A pause as they watch in horror.)* Look at
    her throw! How could anybody grow up and throw like
    that!
BEEZUS *(shaking her head sympathetically).* No kidding.
HENRY. Hey, Mom!
MRS. HUGGINS *(coming up onstage).* Henry! Where have
    you been?
HENRY. I went for a ride in a bathtub.
MRS. HUGGINS. A bathtub?!
HENRY. It's a long story. How come *you're* delivering my
    papers?
MRS. HUGGINS. There wasn't anyone else to do it.
HENRY. Gee, Mom, did you count them out right?
MRS. HUGGINS. Mr. Capper had to count them for you.
HENRY. Oh. Well, I'll take over now. Thanks.
MRS. HUGGINS *(icily).* You're welcome. *(She hands him
    the remaining papers, stalks into the house, calling RIBSY
    after her. MR. CAPPER crosses to HENRY.)*
MR. CAPPER. Henry! There you are! Aren't those papers de-
    livered yet?
HENRY. No, sir, I—
MR. CAPPER. Well, hop to it. People want their news on
    time.
HENRY. I'll deliver them right away.
MR. CAPPER. You do that. Can't always have your mother
    doing the work for you.

HENRY. Yes, sir—I mean, no, sir.

MR. CAPPER. See that you're on time tomorrow, son.

HENRY. Yes, sir. *(MR. CAPPER exits. HENRY goes to get his bike.)* I'll never get these delivered on time.

BEEZUS. I'll help you, Henry.

HENRY. Thanks, Beezus.

MR. HUGGINS *(crosses to HENRY)*. Hello, Henry.

HENRY. Hi, Dad.

MR. HUGGINS. I understand your mother had to take over your route today.

HENRY. Yeah, and golly, you should see her throw. It's pretty awful.

MR. HUGGINS. She was covering for *you*. Something she shouldn't have to do. Henry, that route is your responsibility—nobody else's. That means you do all the work yourself. If you can't, then you'll have to give the route to someone else. Understood?

HENRY. Uh-huh.

MR. HUGGINS. All right, now finish up and head straight inside to change. We're taking your mother out to dinner.

HENRY. Yes, sir.

MR. HUGGINS. And Henry? Instead of giving her pitching tips, you might try thanking her.

HENRY. I will. *(MR. HUGGINS exits.)* Some paperboy I turned out to be. Why'd I want to ride in a stupid ol' bathtub anyway?

*(SCOOTER rides by on his bike.)*

SCOOTER. Hey, Huggins! Hope your mom didn't hit any windows with those papers! I knew a little ol' fifth-grader couldn't handle a paper route. *(He rides off.)*

BEEZUS. Big show-off!

## SCENE TWO

*(School has started. Music up. RIBSY enters. MARY JANE and LISA cross to RIBSY and pat him, etc. ROBERT joins them. JOE the paperboy walks JUDY home. The other PAPERBOYS meet up with him. HENRY, dressed as a crossing guard, helps children cross into the audience. MRS. PEABODY enters, crosses to the Huggins' house and meets MRS. HUGGINS. Both are dressed to go out. HENRY signals MARY JANE, LISA, ROBERT, who cross into audience and up aisle as BEEZUS and RAMONA enter. HENRY signals BEEZUS and RAMONA. As they cross into audience, RAMONA stops to salute HENRY. RIBSY pesters HENRY as he tries to do his job. MRS. HUGGINS and MRS. PEABODY cross down to HENRY. He signals them to cross. As they do so, MRS. HUGGINS stops and kisses him on the cheek. The PAPERBOYS tease him. Music out as MR. CAPPER enters the garage with a stack of papers. The PAPERBOYS count out their papers. HENRY exits to his house, re-enters with his* Journal *bag, without his crossing guard equipment.)*

SCOOTER. How're the headlines today, Mr. Capper?

MR. CAPPER. A newsman's dream, young man.

SCOOTER. That oughta sell papers. Say, Mr. Capper—I'll be needing one more paper after today.

MR. CAPPER. Is that so? Found a new subscriber, have you?

SCOOTER. That's right.

MR. CAPPER. Good for you! Suppose you tell us how you went about selling that subscription.

SCOOTER. Aw, it was easy. I just told this man what a good paper the *Journal* was and he said he didn't have time to read it because he went fishing every Sunday, and I said,

"You could use it to wrap your fish eggs in," and he laughed and said OK, put him down for a subscription, so I did.

MR. CAPPER. I call that quick thinking on your part, Scooter. The rest of you boys could take a lesson from Scooter. *(PAPERBOYS grumble.)* What about you, Henry? You haven't turned in any subscriptions yet.

HENRY. Well...I—I've been trying.

MR. CAPPER. You can't let sales scare you, son. The first one is always the toughest. You've just got to grit your teeth. How about asking Mrs. Peabody?

HENRY. I'll try, sir. But...

MR. CAPPER. No buts about it, my boy. You just march right up to that front door and ring the doorbell. *(He pats HENRY heartily on the back.)* All right, men! Get out there and keep the people informed! You know, the headlines can't wait!

PAPERBOYS. Yes, sir! *(MR. CAPPER and PAPERBOYS exit. HENRY picks up his bag of papers.)*

HENRY *(doing his best MR. CAPPER imitation).* "March right up and ring that doorbell." "Good afternoon. I am your newsboy. I deliver the *Journal* to a lot of your neighbors. I—um—" Let's see—talk about some part of the paper they're interested in. How am I supposed to know what they're interested in? What if I tell them about the church section and all they read are the funny papers?

*(BEEZUS and RAMONA enter. RAMONA is wearing a cardboard tube around her neck, hanging from a piece of string.)*

BEEZUS. Hi, Henry.

HENRY. Hi, Beezus. What are you doing?

BEEZUS. Keeping Ramona away from the TV—what else?

RAMONA *(holding the paper tube in front of her mouth and acting very falsely self-conscious).* My name is Danny Fitzsimmons.

HENRY. It is not. You aren't even a boy.

BEEZUS. She's pretending to be interviewed on the Sheriff Bud show. That's her microphone. *(HENRY starts toward Mrs. Peabody's. RAMONA follows closely behind, trying to step on his heels.)*

RAMONA *(as a running monologue, with HENRY and BEEZUS speaking over her and interrupting).* My name is Danny Fitzsimmons and I want to say hello to my mommy and my daddy and my sister Vicki, who is having a birthday, and Miss Binney, who is my kindergarten teacher, and Lisa Kelly, who is my best friend—

HENRY. Oh, for Pete's sake! Why don't you just say hello to the whole world and be done with it?

RAMONA *(following HENRY).* —and Gloria Lofton, whose cat just had kittens and she might give me one, and her dog Skipper and all the boys and girls in my kindergarten class and all the boys and girls at Glenwood School—

HENRY. STOP FOLLOWING ME!!

RAMONA. —and Georgie Bacon's sister Angela, but I won't say hello to Georgie, because I don't like him, and—

BEEZUS. Ramona be quiet! *(HENRY rings Mrs. Peabody's doorbell.)*

RAMONA. —and Bobby Brogden who has a loose tooth—

BEEZUS. Ramona!

*(Sounds of dog barking. The following dialogue happens almost all at once, very rapidly, with some of it overlapping. MRS. PEABODY enters from back gate, leaving it open.)*

MRS. PEABODY. Yes? *(Dog barking. MRS. PEABODY shouts in the direction of the barking—the side of the house.)* Quiet, Ranger! *(RIBSY also begins barking.)*

HENRY. Ribsy! Quiet! *(RIBSY exits through the back gate.)*

MRS. PEABODY. Oh my goodness, Ranger's back there! *(HENRY and MRS. PEABODY exit through the gate, chasing after RIBSY and yelling.)*

HENRY. Ribsy! Cut it out, you two!

BEEZUS. DOGFIGHT!! *(A crowd gathers to see what's happening. Lots of yelling, ad libs, as follows:)*

MURPH. Who's winning?

ROBERT. I can't tell.

BEEZUS. Henry, watch out!

ROBERT. Go get him, Ribs!

JOE. Somebody throw some water on them!

*(MR. CAPPER hands MR. HUGGINS a bucket. MR. HUGGINS breaks through the crowd, exits by back gate with the bucket. A splash is heard, followed by a moment of stunned silence, then a general gasp. The crowd parts as MRS. PEABODY re-enters, drenched with water. MR. HUGGINS, HENRY and RIBSY follow her. RIBSY exits through doghouse. MR. HUGGINS crosses to MRS. HUGGINS. RAMONA marches up to MRS. PEABODY.)*

RAMONA *(fiercely pointing at MRS. PEABODY)*. Remember, only *you* can prevent forest fires.

BEEZUS. Don't pay any attention to her.

MRS. PEABODY *(dazed)*. Yes, well, indeed. Thank you. *(She exits. The rest of the crowd begins to disperse.)*

RAMONA *(marching up to MR. and MRS. HUGGINS, pointing)*. Only *you* can prevent forest fires!

BEEZUS. Ramona! *(She exits, dragging RAMONA with her. MR. and MRS. HUGGINS shake their heads and exit into house.)*

HENRY. Oh, brother! I can see it now—"No, Mr. Capper, I didn't get that subscription. Why? Well, Ramona was pretending to be on TV and then there was a dogfight and Mrs. Peabody got soaked and then Ramona practically accused her of going around setting forest fires." That Ramona is the biggest pest in the whole neighborhood! *(He exits into his house.)*

## SCENE THREE

*(Music up. MR. HUGGINS enters, looking dejected. He sits on the porch smoking his pipe. MRS. HUGGINS enters and coaxes him into practicing the mambo with her. They dance on the porch, down the steps and back up again. MR. CAPPER, ROGER, ROBERT, MURPH and SEAN enter variously, watch the HUGGINS and exit. Music out as MR. and MRS. HUGGINS exit. HENRY enters pulling a wagon full of lumber. RIBSY enters from doghouse. ROBERT and MURPH enter, cross to HENRY.)*

ROBERT. Wow! Where'd all the lumber come from?

HENRY. From Mr. Grumbie. There's another load after this.

ROBERT. What are you gonna do with it?

HENRY. Build a new doghouse for Ribsy.

MURPH. There's way too much lumber here for just a doghouse—you could build a whole *clubhouse* with all this. *(Reaction from RIBSY.)*

ROBERT. A whole clubhouse! Wow!

MURPH. But when you build a house, you've got to have a plan. You can't just build it any old way.

HENRY. C'mon, Murph—where are we gonna get a plan?

ROBERT. Yeah.

MURPH *(staring them down)*. I'll draw one. This weekend.

*(RAMONA comes racing across the stage with a petticoat on her head.)*

RAMONA *(yelling at the top of her voice)*. Here comes the bride! Here comes the bride!

BEEZUS *(racing after her across the stage)*. RAMONA! RA-MONA GERALDINE QUIMBY, you come back here! *(RIBSY exits.)*

MURPH. But when we get the clubhouse built, NO GIRLS ALLOWED.

HENRY. Aw, Murph—

MURPH *(with a warning look)*. No—girls—allowed.

HENRY & ROBERT *(less heartily than MURPH)*. No girls allowed.

*(MR. HUGGINS enters from his house.)*

MR. HUGGINS. What are you boys up to out here? Storming the Bastille?

ROBERT. Nope. Building a clubhouse! Henry got a bunch of lumber from Mr. Grumbie. And there's another whole load to go.

MR. HUGGINS. You don't say.

HENRY. Don't worry, Dad. I'll saw up the leftover boards for kindling.

MR. HUGGINS. Looks like you've taken on a pretty big job, Henry.

HENRY. Murph's gonna draw up a plan.

MR. HUGGINS. Don't forget, you've still got your paper route to keep up with. AND subscriptions to sell.

HENRY. The clubhouse won't be much trouble—not with all three of us working on it.

ROBERT & MURPH. Yeah.

HENRY. I won't let it get in the way of my route, Dad. Cross my heart.

MR. HUGGINS. I hope you're right. Remember, your mother and I *aren't* going to cover for you.

HENRY. I know, I know. It'll be fine.

MR. HUGGINS. We'll see. You'd better pick up that last load of lumber while Mr. Grumbie's still in a generous mood. *(MR. HUGGINS exits.)*

ROBERT. Come on! *(He races off. HENRY and MURPH remain.)*

MURPH. Cheer up, Henry. If you can handle Ramona, you can handle anything. *(Sound of dog barking. HENRY and MURPH glance over at Mrs. Peabody's yard.)*

HENRY. Yeah. Except Mrs. Peabody's dog.

MURPH. Don't worry, it'll be a breeze once we have a plan. *(They exit together.)*


## SCENE FOUR

*(Halloween evening on Klickitat street. Fun, spooky music up. MRS. PEABODY, MR. CAPPER and MR. and MRS. HUGGINS put up Halloween decorations, exit. Kids go trick-or-treating through the aisles and to the houses. RA-MONA races ahead of the other kids, saying "Trick or treat, smell my feet, give me something good to eat." After two groups of the younger children have come and gone,*

*MR. and MRS. HUGGINS enter to look at the decorations. Two PAPERBOYS enter, wearing ugly masks, and scare RIBSY, who has been watching from in front of his doghouse. PAPERBOYS cross to Mrs. Peabody's and ring doorbell. MRS. PEABODY enters with a really scary mask and scares the PAPERBOYS. PAPERBOYS exit. MR. and MRS. HUGGINS laugh and exit. Music out as HENRY enters, dressed as a Native American. He stands with arms crossed.)*

HENRY. Come, wolf dog!

*(HENRY opens door. RIBSY enters, a wolf mask on his face. MURPH and ROBERT enter. MURPH wears a space alien disguise. The eyes on his spaceman head light up. ROBERT is dressed as a cowboy.)*

MURPH *(holding out his hand to HENRY)*. Greetings, earthling.

HENRY *(shakes hands with him and gets a buzzer shock)*. Yipe! Is that you, Murph?

MURPH *(blinking his spaceman eyes on and off)*. Affirmative.

*(BEEZUS, as a gypsy, and RAMONA, as a devil, enter. RAMONA runs ahead, reaching HENRY first.)*

RAMONA. I got a Nutsie candy bar! "Nutsies give both children and adults quick energy. Avoid that mid-afternoon slump with a Nutsie, chock-full of protein-rich nuts!"

HENRY. Gosh! What does she do—memorize commercials?

BEEZUS. Yup.

MURPH *(to BEEZUS)*. Greetings, earthling. *(He holds out his hand to her.)*

HENRY. Watch out, Beezus!

BEEZUS. I'm not falling for your ol' trick, Murph. I've been warned. *(MURPH buzzes in HENRY's direction, disappointed. BEEZUS addresses HENRY.)* Stay away from the people on the corner, Henry. They told us to do a trick.

RAMONA. I sang a little song for them. *(Sings.)* "Crispy Potato Chips are the best, North or South, East or West. Crispy Potato Chips, hooray, hooray! Get your Crispy Chips today."

BEEZUS *(disgusted)*. The people thought it was cute.

RAMONA. It's a nice song. I like it. *(She starts singing again as she skips offstage.)*

BEEZUS *(calling to HENRY as she follows after RAMONA)*. Mrs. Peabody's giving out candy apples. Ramona, come back here!

ROBERT. Candy apples?! Come on!

HENRY. I don't know...

MURPH. You're not still afraid of her dog, are you?

HENRY. No.

MURPH. You are!

HENRY. I am not! Come on. *(They march over to Mrs. Peabody's. HENRY halts nervously; to MURPH.)* You ring it.

*(MURPH rings the doorbell. MRS. PEABODY answers.)*

HENRY, ROBERT & MURPH. Trick or treat! *(There is a bark, then a whining from inside the house.)*

MRS. PEABODY. Gracious, Ranger! It's just Harry and his friends dressed up for trick-or-treat. Come out from under the couch. They won't bite. *(ROBERT and MURPH take candy apples and sit on Mrs. Peabody's steps.)*

HENRY. Mrs. Peabody, I-I'm sorry about the dogfight and you getting soaked and what Ramona said about not causing forest fires.

MRS. PEABODY (*laughing*). Oh, children and pets! Here, have a candy apple.

HENRY. Thanks. (*Clearing his throat.*) Um—I deliver the *Journal* to many of your neighbors. The Sunday supplement has a good column about pets you might enjoy...I thought...maybe...you might want a subscription?

MRS. PEABODY. Well, it's about time. I've been waiting for you to come and sell me one.

HENRY. You have?

MRS. PEABODY. Yes, I have. I thought you might want to get credit for a subscription.

ROBERT. Oh, he does! (*HENRY gives ROBERT a look.*)

MRS. PEABODY. It took you so long I was about to give up and call the paper myself. Now, don't you worry about my new dog. Ranger felt like he had to defend his property, but now that he sees we're friends, he'll be all right. He's really just a lamb.

HENRY. Well...uh...thanks a lot for the subscription. And the candy apple. I'll start leaving you a paper tomorrow.

MRS. PEABODY. Good! I've missed the antiques column. Good night, Harry. (*She exits.*)

ROBERT & MURPH. Harry?!

HENRY. At least I got the subscription.

ROBERT & MURPH. Yeah, *Harry!*

HENRY. Race ya to the next house! (*The BOYS race off.*)

## SCENE FIVE

*(Music up. MR. and MRS. HUGGINS, MRS. PEABODY
and MR. CAPPER take down their Halloween decorations.
MR. HUGGINS gives RIBSY a bone. RIBSY tries to bury it
in MRS. PEABODY's flowerbeds. She chases him away,
exits. PAPERBOYS begin bringing on pieces of the clubhouse and assembling it between the Huggins' and the
Capper's houses. ROBERT and MURPH enter. MURPH
carries blueprints, ROBERT carries a box of tools. They
supervise the construction of the clubhouse as RIBSY tries
to bury his bone in Mr. Capper's front lawn. MR. CAPPER
chases him away and exits. RIBSY finally gives the bone to
an audience member and exits. Music out as MR. HUG-
GINS re-enters, scrutinizes the construction of the clubhouse. PAPERBOYS exit as soon as the clubhouse pieces
are assembled.)*

MURPH. What do you think, Mr. Huggins?

MR. HUGGINS. Not bad. Not bad at all.

ROBERT. Murph designed the plans himself.

MR. HUGGINS. So I've been told.

MURPH. Where's Henry? We need his help for the finishing
touches.

MR. HUGGINS. He had a little trouble collecting money
from his newspaper customers. He'll be back soon. Make
yourselves at home.

*(He exits. ROBERT and MURPH begin "painting" the
clubhouse. BEEZUS enters, carrying cans of paint. RA-
MONA trails behind her.)*

BEEZUS. Looks like you're almost done.

ROBERT. Yup.

BEEZUS. Where's Henry?

ROBERT. Collecting from his customers.

BEEZUS. Well, I brought some extra paint we had in our basement. I thought you might need to paint the clubhouse before the weather gets too cold. *(She hands the paint cans to MURPH.)*

ROBERT *(with a look to MURPH)*. Um...thanks.

MURPH. We'll be using wood stain. We don't need any paint. *(He gives the paint cans back to BEEZUS. She puts them down by the Huggins' steps. RAMONA begins "painting" the Huggins' porch.)*

BEEZUS. Do you want help pounding the nails while Henry's gone?

MURPH. No.

ROBERT. You can stay and watch if you want.

*(MURPH gives him a look—HENRY enters, out of breath.)*

HENRY. Sorry it took me so long. I had to go back to Mrs. Kelly's house twice. *(Noticing BEEZUS.)* Hi, Beezus.

BEEZUS. Hi, Henry.

RAMONA. How is a dog different from a flea?

HENRY *(grudgingly)*. I don't know. How?

RAMONA. Dogs can have fleas but fleas can't have dogs! *(She laughs. HENRY groans, starts working on the clubhouse.)* Why did the chicken cross the road?

MURPH. Go home!

RAMONA. To get to the other side! *(Again, she laughs herself silly. RAMONA runs to the top step of the Huggins' porch. Rapidly.)* Ten, nine, eight, seven, six, five, four, three, two, one, BLAST OFF! *(She jumps off the porch.)*

BEEZUS. Ramona, stop being such a pest.

RAMONA. Can we have some nails to take home?

ROBERT. No.

RAMONA. Why not?

MURPH. No girls allowed. *(Prompting HENRY.)* Right, Henry?

HENRY *(sheepishly)*. Right.

BEEZUS. That's not fair.

MURPH. Get lost. *(BEEZUS looks at HENRY.)*

HENRY. No girls allowed, Beezus.

BEEZUS. Well, all right for you, smarties! *(She storms off. RAMONA sticks her tongue out at HENRY, then marches off after BEEZUS.)*

MURPH. Pesky girls! *(As the boys work, MURPH starts chanting at lightning speed.)*

> Fadatta. Fadatta.
>
> Fadatta beepum boopum bah!
>
> Ratta datta boom, shhhh!
>
> Ahfah deedee bobo.

ROBERT. Say that again, Murph—only a whole lot slower.

MURPH. Fadatta. Fadatta.

> Fadatta beepum boopum bah.
>
> Ratta datta boom Shh-!
>
> Ahfah deedee bobo.

*(The other BOYS repeat it. They say it again, together, faster.)*

HENRY. Hey! We could use that for a secret password!

ROBERT. Yeah! We'll say it so fast the other kids can't learn it. And we won't teach it to them!

MURPH. Especially girls.

HENRY, MURPH & ROBERT. Fadatta. Fadatta.

> Fadatta beepum boopum bah.
>
> Ratta datta boom Shh-!
>
> Ahfah deeded bobo!

*(They step back to admire their work on the clubhouse.)*

MURPH. Finished. Solid as a rock.

HENRY. Now for the final touch. *(He goes into his house.)*

MURPH. What final touch?

ROBERT. How should I know?

MURPH. It better not mess up my plans!

*(HENRY re-enters with a large stuffed owl. He places it in a prominent spot.)*

HENRY. Tadaa!

ROBERT. Spooky!

MURPH. Where'd you get it—Mrs. Peabody?

HENRY. How did you guess?

ROBERT. Hey, let's go to my house—my dad has some extra crates we could use for furniture.

*(MRS. HUGGINS comes out on the porch.)*

MRS. HUGGINS. Henry! Be sure you clean up when you're finished out there!

ROBERT & MURPH. Yes, Mrs. Huggins.

*(HENRY, ROBERT and MURPH gather up some of their supplies and take them offstage. Spy music plays as BEEZUS sneaks on, looks around to be sure the BOYS are gone. She puts a doll's bonnet on the owl and sticks a rolled-up piece of paper in its mouth so it looks like it's smoking a cigarette. She hides as the BOYS re-enter, and the spy music fades out. HENRY, ROBERT & MURPH ad-lib about how they'll set up the inside of the clubhouse. Then they spot the owl.).*

HENRY, ROBERT & MURPH. Hey!

ROBERT. How do you like that! I'll bet old Beezus did this.

MURPH. That does it. *(He grabs a can of leftover paint and a leftover board and "paints" a sign reading THIS MEANS YOU which he hangs on the clubhouse. The signs can all be pre-painted. Actors can mime painting. The clubhouse already has the words NO GIRLS ALLOWED painted on the side.)*

HENRY, ROBERT & MURPH. NO GIRLS ALLOWED— THIS MEANS YOU!

MURPH. That oughta tell her not to mess with us.

*(They take another batch of boxes/supplies offstage. HENRY removes the doll's bonnet and "cigarette" from the owl. The BOYS exit. Spy music as BEEZUS sneaks out, "paints" and hangs a sign on the owl reading DOWN WITH BOYS. She hides. Music out. The boys re-enter, ad-libbing, and see the owl.)*

HENRY. I don't believe it!

ROBERT. The nerve of some people.

MURPH. That's a girl for you.

HENRY. Huddle up. *(They form a semi-circle C.)* We need a lock.

MURPH. A padlock.

ROBERT. With a key.

HENRY. I'll bet if we pool our money we can get one down at the hardware store. Come on!

*(They count their change and exit, running. Spy music up as BEEZUS sneaks out, paints and hangs a new sign on the clubhouse—HA, HA, YOU THINK YOU ARE SMART—and exits. Music out. The boys return with the padlock and keys.)*

HENRY. She got us again!

MURPH *(taking down the latest sign)*. Well, she won't get us anymore. *(They put the owl inside and put the padlock an the clubhouse.)* There.

HENRY. We can't all have a key—the lock only comes with two keys.

ROBERT. Maybe we could have a secret hiding place. *(They look over their shoulders to be sure BEEZUS isn't listening.)*

HENRY. How about under Mrs. Peabody's flower pot?

MURPH & ROBERT. Good idea. *(One boy hides the key while the other two cover him.)*

ROBERT. What about the other key?

MURPH. Under the doormat on Henry's front porch. *(They hide the second key, using the same method.)* Now, swear on your honor not to tell *anybody* the hiding spot. *(To HENRY.)* Especially a girl.

HENRY, ROBERT & MURPH *(solemnly raise their hands)*. On my honor I swear. *(They do a secret handshake.)*

MURPH. That should fix old Beezus.


## SCENE SIX

*(Music up. ROGER enters, crosses to clubhouse. HENRY, ROBERT and MURPH show off the clubhouse. MARY JANE and LISA enter. HENRY, ROBERT and MURPH chase them away. JOE, the paperboy, walks JUDY home from school. HENRY exits to his house. ROBERT and MURPH exit together. BEEZUS and RAMONA enter, look at clubhouse, whisper together, exit. Music out as HENRY enters from his house. He begins daydreaming, using the clubhouse as a spaceship.)*

HENRY *(getting the key from the doormat and unlocking the clubhouse)*. Here he is, ladies and gentlemen—the First Paper Boy in Space. The folks back at his hometown paper must be proud of this young man. *(HENRY replaces the key, steps into the clubhouse.)* He's suited up and ready to board the rocket ship. All systems are go.

*(RAMONA enters.)*

RAMONA. Hello.

HENRY *(turns, bonks his head on clubhouse roof, startled)*. Oh...hi. Where's Beezus?

RAMONA. Home.

HENRY *(suspicious)*. Why didn't she come with you?

RAMONA. Because you are mean to her.

HENRY *(uncomfortable)*. Well, boys have a right to do things without girls around. Why don't you go home?

RAMONA. I don't want to. *(HENRY sighs in exasperation and goes into the clubhouse. RAMONA closes the door behind him and locks the padlock. HENRY turns and struggles with the door, realizes it's locked.)*

HENRY. Hey! Let me out of here!

RAMONA. I don't have a key.

HENRY *(kicks and bangs on the walls)*. Help! Help! H-E-L-L-P!!!!

RAMONA. Huh-huh-huh-help—*(Proudly.)* Help starts with an H!

HENRY. Let me out! *(He slumps in frustration.)* My paper route! I can't be trapped in here or I won't get the papers delivered! *(RAMONA has begun to wander away, her attention elsewhere.)* Ramona! Wait! *(She stops and looks at him.)* Come here. I want to tell you a secret. A big secret. A secret that only *boys* know.

RAMONA. I don't like boys. Boys are mean. *(She turns to leave.)*

HENRY. Only three people in the whole world know this secret. *(RAMONA stops again. HENRY takes a deep breath.)* I'm going to tell you where the key to the clubhouse is.

RAMONA. Where?

HENRY. First you have to promise to unlock the padlock.

RAMONA. I don't want to unlock it.

HENRY. But *why?!*

RAMONA. I just don't.

HENRY *(calling for help in desperation).*

    Fadatta. Fadatta.

    Fadatta beepum boopum bah!

    Ratta datta boom Shh-!

    Ahfah deedee bobo!

RAMONA. Say that again, Henry.

HENRY. No.

RAMONA. Please.

HENRY. Promise to unlock the padlock?

RAMONA. Puh-puh-puh-padlock starts with a P!

HENRY. I *know* padlock starts with a P! Now will you get the key? Key starts with a K.

RAMONA. We haven't had K yet at school.

HENRY. Just get the key.

RAMONA. Where is it?

HENRY *(miserable at revealing the secret).* Under the mat on the front porch. *(RAMONA gets the key.)*

RAMONA. Say those words again.

HENRY. Fadatta, fadatta.

    Fadattabeepumboopumbah!RattadattaboomShh-!

    Ahfahdeedeebobo.

Now unlock the padlock.

RAMONA *(tries).* I can't make the key turn.

HENRY. Look, go get Beezus. If you do, I'll teach you both the secret words. *(Pause.)* And—tell Beezus I'm sorry. *(RAMONA exits.)* I am a traitor. A one-hundred percent traitor. But I've got to get my papers delivered. What if Ramona forgets to tell Beezus? What if she plops down in front of the TV and forgets all about me?

*(BEEZUS enters.)*

BEEZUS *(with an edge in her voice)*. Hi, Henry.

HENRY. Hi, Beezus. It's sure nice of you to come and let me out after the way I... uh...acted.

BEEZUS. I didn't say I was going to let you out. You don't want girls around, remember?

HENRY. Aw, come on, Beezus.

BEEZUS. Give me one good reason to let you out.

HENRY. I've got to start my paper route. If I mess up, I'll lose it. Please?

BEEZUS *(after a pause)*. Oh, all right, I'll let you out—but only because you have to start your route. I'm still mad at you. AND you have to teach me the secret words before I let you out.

HENRY. Oh, all right, if that's the way you feel about it. *(He says the secret words. BEEZUS repeats after him, then says it once through on her own.)* NOW will you let me out?

BEEZUS. I suppose so. *(She unlocks the clubhouse and opens the door.)* There.

HENRY. Thanks, Beezus.

BEEZUS. Fadatta, fadatta! *(mischievously.)* I think I'll go teach the secret words to *Ramona*, now. Byyyyye! *(She exits.)*

HENRY. Great. Now the secret words will be all over the neighborhood.

## SCENE SEVEN

*(About a week later. No music. A burst of "Fadatta, fadatta," etc., from rear of theater. CHILDREN and ADULTS enter chanting "Fadatta, fadatta," until at last it reaches a crescendo, then dies out as they exit. HENRY enters.)*

HENRY. That Ramona is such a pest! She keeps messing me up on my paper route. If I don't do something soon, I'll lose my route—or the clubhouse. The problem is, Ramona won't listen to anybody.

*(BEEZUS and RAMONA enter, BEEZUS being dragged towards home by RAMONA. BEEZUS and HENRY look at each other.)*

HENRY. Hi, Beezus.

BEEZUS. Hi, Henry. *(An awkward pause.)* Guess the secret words aren't so secret anymore, huh?

HENRY. That's OK.

BEEZUS. Mother says if she hears one more "fadatta fadatta" she'll scream. *(They both laugh awkwardly. BEEZUS starts to leave.)* Well, so long. *(HENRY stops her.)*

HENRY. Say, Beezus. *(Pause.)* I'm sure sorry about...um... everything.

BEEZUS. Aw, that's okay.

HENRY. Friends? *(Holding out his hand.)*

BEEZUS. Friends. *(They shake hands.)*

RAMONA *(tugging on BEEZUS)*. Come on. Come on or we'll be late for Sheriff Bud.

BEEZUS. I can't understand it. She can't even tell time, but she always knows when it's time for the Sheriff Bud show.

HENRY. Like Ribsy. He can't tell time either, but he always knows when to meet me after school.

RAMONA. Come ON! *(She drags BEEZUS offstage).*

BEEZUS. Okay! Okay! See ya, Henry. *(They exit.)*

HENRY. Sheriff Bud! Ramona never misses his program. If there's anyone she'll listen to, it's Sheriff Bud. *(He thinks for a moment, then exits into his house.)*

SCENE EIGHT

*(Music up. MR. CAPPER and MRS. PEABODY enter to hang Christmas decorations. PAPERBOYS enter, playing football. MR. HUGGINS unexpectedly catches the ball, plows through the PAPERBOYS, jumps up and down at his success, then realizes he's lost his cool. He exits stiffly, tossing the ball to the boys on his way out. They laugh, exit, as do MR. CAPPER and MRS. PEABODY. Music out as MR. HUGGINS re-enters with Christmas lights, humming/singing a holiday tune. HENRY follows with another box of lights. MR. HUGGINS begins hanging the Christmas lights. HENRY works on untangling a string of lights. BEEZUS and RAMONA enter, cross to Huggins house.)*

BEEZUS. Hi, Henry! Hi, Mr. Huggins!

HENRY. Hi, Beezus!

MR. HUGGINS. Hello, Beezus. Ready for a little holiday spirit?

BEEZUS. Sure thing.

RAMONA. Beezus! Beezus! It's time for Sheriff Bud!

BEEZUS *(under her breath as she grabs RAMONA).* Ramona…*(To MR. HUGGINS.)* Would you mind?

MR. HUGGINS. Be my guest. *(RAMONA races inside. BEEZUS joins HENRY in untangling the lights.)*

SHERIFF BUD *(voice-over)*. I want all you little folks out there in TV land to do something for old Sheriff Bud. I want you to tell Mother right now, right this very minute, to put Crispy Potato Chips on her shopping list. The chips guaranteed not to bend.

RAMONA *(races outside)*. Beezus! Sheriff Bud says—

BEEZUS. I don't care what Sheriff Bud says. *(RAMONA goes back inside. BEEZUS pulling HENRY downstage.)* Did you send the letter yet, Henry?

HENRY. Yup! Straight to Sheriff Bud.

BEEZUS. Do you really think he'll read it on TV?

HENRY. I don't know, Beezus. I've been watching the show for days and he hasn't said a word about it.

SHERIFF BUD. And now for today's mail.

BEEZUS. Shhhh! *(She and HENRY race to the door to listen, reacting to what SHERIFF BUD says.)*

SHERIFF BUD. Ramona Geraldine Quimby—I see you out there in TV land. *(Reaction from HENRY and BEEZUS.)*

RAMONA *(squealing from inside)*. He sees me!

SHERIFF BUD. Ramona Geraldine Quimby, I want you to do something that will make old Sheriff Bud very, very happy. Ramona, it will make old Sheriff Bud very, very happy if you stop pestering Henry Huggins on his paper route. Do you promise?

RAMONA. I promise.

SHERIFF BUD. Good. We've got to get those papers delivered. The headlines can't wait.

*(RAMONA enters, wide-eyed. BEEZUS and HENRY pretend nonchalance. RAMONA tugs at HENRY.)*

RAMONA. Do you really know Sheriff Bud?!

HENRY. Well...I guess you might say he's a friend of mine.

BEEZUS. Ramona, you better not pester Henry on his paper route again.

RAMONA. I-I won't do it anymore.

HENRY. Promise?

RAMONA. I promise.

MR. HUGGINS. All right, everybody! Time to test out our handiwork!

HENRY. Hey, Mom! Come and see the lights!

*(MRS. HUGGINS enters.)*

MR. HUGGINS. Stand back! *(He plugs in the lights. The Christmas lights light up and the family admires them. All exit inside Huggins house.)*

### SCENE NINE

*(Christmas time on Klickitat Street. Holiday music up. MRS. PEABODY brings fruitcake to the Huggins house. PAPERBOYS, one by one, bring presents for JUDY. MR. CAPPER answers the door each time, takes the present. PAPERBOYS wait in a line for JUDY. SCOOTER arrives last, wearing a tuxedo jacket and carrying a corsage. Finally JUDY enters in a prom dress. SCOOTER gives her the corsage and they exit together, to the disappointment of the PAPERBOYS. MRS. PEABODY crosses to MR. CAPPER, gives him the fruitcake. He gives her a box of candy brought by one of the PAPERBOYS and intended for JUDY. They exit together. Music out as HENRY enters.)*

HENRY. So much for that bright idea. Now that Ramona thinks I know Sheriff Bud personally, she follows me everywhere. The worst part is—she behaves herself.

*(He arrives at Mr. Capper's garage. MR. CAPPER enters, gives PAPERBOYS their papers. BEEZUS enters.)*

BEEZUS. Henry, I don't think you're going to like what Ramona got for Christmas.

HENRY. Oh, no—what did she get?

*(RAMONA comes bounding up, an obviously homemade* Journal *bag over her shoulders).*

RAMONA. Henry, see what Santa brought me? Now I can be a paperboy, just like you. *(The PAPERBOYS laugh and tease HENRY.)*

BEEZUS *(to HENRY).* Sorry, Henry. It was the only thing she wanted for Christmas. I tried to warn you.

HENRY. Thanks, anyway.

MR. CAPPER. Well, well, Henry. Looks like you've got yourself a little shadow.

HENRY *(not thrilled).* Yes, sir.

MR. CAPPER *(to RAMONA).* So, little lady, you're looking to join the news business?

RAMONA. I want to be a paperboy—just like Henry. *(The other PAPERBOYS laugh again. MR. CAPPER cuts them off with a look.)*

MR. CAPPER. Young ambition is no laughing matter.

PAPERBOYS. Yes, sir.

MR. CAPPER *(to JOE).* This young lady could be delivering papers to you one day. *(A few snorts and giggles from the PAPERBOYS.)*

JOE. Uh... yes, sir.

MR. CAPPER. Now enough chit-chat. Get those papers delivered! Y'know, the headlines can't wait! *(All exit.)*


## SCENE TEN

*(Snow effect. Mirror ball dapples the ceiling with spinning light as holiday music plays and the following radio voice-over is heard.)*

RADIO ANNOUNCER *(voice-over).* Take a look out your window this morning, folks! There's over a foot of snow out there today. We have traffic buildups throughout the city as holiday travelers take to the highways. The roads are slippery, so drive carefully. Or just stay home and cuddle up with your sweetie. The Colossal Supermarket is offering Blizzard Bargains on tire chains and anti-freeze. Plus free candy-canes for the kiddies—and poinsettias for the ladies. Get out those snow shovels and bundle up! It's one for the record books!

*(Music and radio out. Lights up, revealing large styrofoam snowdrifts onstage. MRS. PEABODY's flowers are gone. RAMONA enters, wearing her* Journal *bag. HENRY follows, pulling a sled full of newspapers. He doesn't have his bike.)*

RAMONA. There's an easy house number—*(Slowly, intently.)* "Three-Two-Three-Three."

HENRY. It's getting cold, Ramona—why don't you go home?

RAMONA. No. I want to be a paperboy like you.

HENRY. Can't you be a paperboy some other day?

RAMONA. You ride your bike all the other days. I won't pester you.

HENRY. You better not.

*(HENRY rings Mrs. Peabody's doorbell and MRS. PEA-BODY answers, He hands her the newspaper.)*

MRS. PEABODY. Why, it's Harry Higgins! What a thoughtful boy to bring the paper right up to the front door!

RAMONA. His name isn't Harry Higgins! It's *Henry Huggins! (She sits on MRS. PEABODY's porch steps.)*

MRS. PEABODY *(to HENRY).* Is it really?

HENRY. Well...yes.

MRS. PEABODY. I am so sorry. To think that I've been calling you Harry Higgins all this time. *(She laughs.)* I don't see how I could have made such a mistake.

HENRY. Aw, I knew who you meant.

RAMONA. My feet are cold.

MRS. PEABODY. Poor little thing.

RAMONA. I'm tired.

HENRY. Aw, come on, Ramona. I'm almost done with my route.

RAMONA. I want to go home—NOW! *(She breaks into tears.)*

MRS. PEABODY. She's all worn out. If I could get my car out of the garage I would drive her home myself.

HENRY *(reluctantly, looking first at his sled, then at RA-MONA).* Come on, Ramona. Get on the sled and I'll pull you home. *(He puts RAMONA on the sled.)* Now, hang on. *(He begins pulling the sled. RAMONA stops crying.)*

RAMONA. Mush! Mush!

HENRY. Aw, keep quiet! *(They exit.)*

## SCENE ELEVEN

*(New Year's Eve. The snow is still on the ground. Music up. The PAPERBOYS arrive in a particularly rowdy mood, roughhousing in the snow. MR. and MRS. HUGGINS enter from the audience, dressed up to go out. They get caught in the middle of a snowball fight with the PAPERBOYS and good-naturedly join in for a moment before escaping into the house. Music out as MR. CAPPER enters with the papers, then begins reading one. HENRY enters. During the ensuing lines, the rest of the neighborhood gathers to hear what has happened.)*

MR. CAPPER. Well, Henry. I see you got your name in the paper.

HENRY. Who, me?

MR. CAPPER. Yes, you, young man. Right here on the editorial page.

HENRY. The editorial page? It must be some other Henry Huggins.

MR. CAPPER. I don't think so. *(Gets all the PAPERBOYS' attention and reads from the paper, proudly.)* "Dear Editor—I wish to call attention to the fine work a boy named Henry Huggins is doing delivering the *Journal* in our neighborhood."

HENRY. Hey, that *is* me!

MR. CAPPER. I told you. "Henry is always prompt and courteous, but yesterday during the heavy snow I was particularly impressed. Henry went out of his way to hand me my paper in person so that it would not get buried in a snowdrift. He also took time out from his route to give a cold, tired little girl a ride home on his sled. The *Journal* should be proud of this fine young citizen. Sincerely, Bessie Peabody."

BEEZUS. Congratulations, Henry!

MURPH. Good job, Henry!

MAX. Boy! I wish somebody would write a letter like that about me!

JOE. Me, too. I've been delivering papers for three years and nobody ever wrote a letter like that about me.

SEAN. Me neither.

MR. CAPPER. AND—Henry is our youngest carrier.

SCOOTER. Say, Henry. I guess a fifth-grader can handle a paper route after all. *(He shakes hands with HENRY.)*

MR. CAPPER. Keep up the good work, Henry. Rain or sleet or snow, as they say. You're one fine news carrier. *(General cheering.)* Now, let's get those papers delivered! You know—

ALL. The headlines can't wait!

MR. CAPPER. That's the truth, you know.

*(MR. CAPPER exits and the PAPERBOYS disperse, congratulating HENRY. RIBSY, MR. and MRS. HUGGINS enter. HENRY races to his house.)*

HENRY. Mom! Dad!

MRS. HUGGINS. What is it, Henry?

HENRY. I got my name in the newspaper! On the editorial page!

MR. HUGGINS. The editorial page?

HENRY. There. *(He hands them a paper. They read together.)*

MRS. HUGGINS. Henry! Good for you! *(She goes inside the house for Mr. Huggins' coat.)*

MR. HUGGINS. Well, I'll tell you, Henry, when you took on the paper route and then got mixed up in the clubhouse, I didn't think you could handle it. But you've done a good job.

*(He pats HENRY on the back. MRS. HUGGINS brings MR. HUGGINS' coat.)*

MR. HUGGINS. I don't care how much snow there is. I'm going right out to buy an extra dozen papers—copies for everyone! *(MR. HUGGINS exits.)*

MRS. HUGGINS. I'll go call the grandparents! I'm very proud of you, Henry. *(She kisses HENRY on the forehead and exits.)*

HENRY *(to RIBSY).* I guess I'm pretty important after all. Good old Mrs. Peabody. You know, Ribs, if it wasn't for Ramona, Mrs. Peabody would've written to the *Journal* about some boy named *Harry Higgins.* If it wasn't for Ramona, I wouldn't have gotten you untrained so I could take Scooter's route. And if Ramona didn't bug poor old Murph, I wouldn't have gotten my *own* paper route anyway.

*(RAMONA comes skipping along, slips and falls. HENRY helps her up.)*

HENRY *(to RAMONA).* Be careful and don't fall again. You might get hurt. *(He smiles as RAMONA skips off.)* Good ol' Ramona. *(RIBSY jumps up, knocks HENRY down, licks his face as lights go to black.)*

END OF PLAY

## PRODUCTION NOTES

### PERIOD

The original production of *Henry Huggins* was set in the 1950s, but Beverly Cleary's characters and stories are timeless. With only minor changes, the play could take place in almost any era. Most of the script was based on the books Henry and Beezus, Henry and the Paper Route and Henry and the Clubhouse. Louis Darling's charming illustrations provided in these three books are excellent references for costume, set and props details.

### SET

Klickitat Street. Three house fronts—Mrs. Peabody's, Henry's and Mr. Capper's. All three houses have some sort of front porch. There are two chairs on the Huggins' porch. There is a back gate between the Huggins' and Mrs. Peabody's. Ribsy's doghouse is in front of the Huggins'. A clubhouse is assembled onstage during one of the scenes. The original production took place on a wide, thrust stage. It may not always be practical to have all three house fronts onstage at once. For other spaces, you may need to use a different set design.

Set dressing includes seasonal outdoor decorations (specifically Christmas lights and decorations, Halloween, Fourth of July) and birthday party decorations. The final few scenes call for snow on the ground. The snow doesn't need to fall from the sky.

### TRANSITIONAL SCENES

There are short transition scenes between the main scenes of the play. The transitions help give a sense of continuity, create the community atmosphere of Klickitat Street, establish the seasons and flesh out some of the minor characters. The transitions have no discernible dialogue and should be accompanied by music. The transitions should last a minute or two at most. The script includes fairly detailed stage descriptions for these transitions, but the details are less important that the "flavor" of the scene.

## MUSIC

In the original production, light, nostalgic dance music from the late '40s and '50s was used with wonderful effect. There is an innocent quality to this post-swing/pre-rock era music that perfectly fit the feel of the show. The Huggins' "mambo" lessons and Judy's jitterbug with the Paperboys added special insight into these characters.

## CAST SIZE

The original production included the characters of Roger, Lisa and Mary Jane. These children understudied the roles of Henry, Ramona and Beezus respectively, and added neighborhood flavor, but are not essential and can be easily cut. The number of Paperboys can also be adapted to suit the needs of any given production.

## PARTIAL PROPS LIST

Bathtub on dolly, bags for newspapers, wires/etc. for Thorvo, the robot. A sled, a variety of garage sale odds and ends. A cardboard tube from a toilet paper roll, Trick-or-Treat bags, a stuffed owl, watering can, 3 squirt guns, 4 umbrellas, school books, crossing guard flag, briefcase, picnic basket, card table, picnic food, cardboard boxes, 2 small American flags.

## BICYCLES

One of the more exciting elements of the original production was the use of actual bicycles by the Paperboys (and eventually Henry). Special ramps were used allowing the boys to ride up and down the aisles and through the theater, delivering newspapers to the audience. While visually spectacular, this stunt requires a *great deal* of practice to be done safely and may not be practical in all performance spaces. Remember, safety must be the deciding factor. Henry, Ramona, Mrs. Huggins and Murph all delivered their papers on foot at times and this, too, had great effect. The newspapers were specially printed up for the production and became wonderful souvenirs for the audience.

## RIBSY & THE KITTENS

The use of live animals in this production is *strongly* discouraged. For the premiere production, an ingenious "body puppet" costume was created for Ribsy, thus allowing the character to be played by a child. The role is physically demanding, but using a live actor allowed Ribsy to participate more fully and creatively in the action of the play. Small stuffed animals were used for the kittens which the actors playing Henry and his parents manipulated to look like they were moving.

## COSTUMES

HENRY: Jeans, shirt, sneakers, sometimes a jacket. Ramona: Overalls, sometimes a dress (for school). BEEZUS: jeans, oxford shirt and loafers, sometimes a skirt and blouse/sweater (for school). RIBSY: Need not be elaborate. May be very simple (as a Halloween dog costume is done). For the suit, perhaps a pair of pajamas with spots sewn onto them, etc.